CAROL'S FANTASTIC UNIVERSE

STARSHIPS, ALIENS, OTHER DIMENSIONS AND SCIENCE FICTION CONCEPTS

Carol Ann Rodriguez

Inner Light - Global Communications

PO Box 753
New Brunswick, NJ 08903

MRUFO8@HOTMAIL.COM

CAROL'S FANTASTIC UNIVERSE

STARSHIPS, ALIENS, OTHER DIMENSIONS AND SCIENCE FICTION CONCEPTS

By Carol Ann Rodriguez

INNER LIGHT/GLOBAL COMMUNICATIONS

CAROL'S FANTASTIC UNIVERSE

STARSHIPS, ALIENS, OTHER DIMENSIONS
AND
SCIENCE FICTION CONCEPTS

By Carol Ann Rodriguez

© 2016 Carol Ann Rodriguez

Published By Timothy Green Beckley

DBA Inner Light/Global Communications - All Rights Reserved

Printed in the United States of America

Timothy Green Beckley: Editorial Director

Carol Ann Rodriguez: Publishers Assistant

Editor & Graphics: Tim R. Swartz

Sean Casteel: Associate Editor

William Kern: Associate Editor & Art Consultant

Email: mrufo8@hotmail.com

Conspiracyjournal.com

YouTube Channel – Mr UFOs Secret Files

Contents

© Carol Ann Rodriguez

A WORD FROM THE PUBLISHER AND COLLEAGUE TIMOTHY G. BECKLEY

For a brief period in 1971, I represented the publisher of Peter Max's Paper Airplane Book. I always loved Peter's use of vibrant colors which often utilized a dazzling "psychedelic" patterns of stars. I personable perceive a similarity in the art of the very talented Carol Ann Rodriguez whose work we are privileged to be premiering in her first art collection.

I have been fortunate to know Carol for many years. I first made her acquaintance through a mutual friend, Walli Elmlark, the "White Witch of New York." Carol was very much interested in the occult and UFOs - especially in anything related to outer space and alien beings. She attended many workshops and lectures at the New York School of Occult Arts and Sciences over which I presided. We hooked up to venture out into the world and traveled to the Yucatan to investigate the possibility of an ancient alien influence on the culture. Carol assisted greatly in the organization and the running of numerous conferences that I organized in several states.

But above all else I was greatly impressed with the dedication and the many hours she put into developing her art work. A major portion of her energies went into the creation of colorful portraits of extraterrestrials, multi-dimensional beings and an occasional character right out of the pages of some horror classic. We used her work in our many publications - *UFO Universe, Front Page Disasters, Angels and Aliens* - you name it. The colors she uses are not duplicated by any other artist on the scene today.

We consider it an honor to be able to publish this portfolio which is our first full color book.

Timothy Green Beckley

As a child I was always interested in the idea of space aliens, far distant worlds, time travel other dimensions and beings that are dreamed about, but we are told could not possibly exist.

To me, the supernatural is very natural. Nothing is too fantastic to be envisaged. I can sometimes close my eyes and "imagine" a vast universe that to most people remains unseen, but to me I am right there among the stars.

I hope I have helped others to see the invisible cosmos hidden all around us. My philosophy is that the main purpose of my art is to decorate a good story or to make a cover "come alive."

Facts and figures are for the writer to adhere to. The illustrator needs to attract attention to a book or an article. My job is to see the future, to explore the past.

I invite you to travel with me to far distant realms where we are free to believe in that which in our everyday lives is often said to be "unrealistic."

Carol,
Bon Voyage From a Galaxy Far, Far Away.

Carol's Fantastic Universe
Copyright © 2016 Carol Ann Rodriguez
All Rights Reserved

Published by Timothy Green Beckley,
dba Inner Light/Global Communications
P.O. Box 753, New Brunswick, NJ 08903

THE CITY SHIP HAS ARRIVED

9

DO THEY COME IN PEACE?

11

STARSEEDS

13

© Carol Ann Rodriguez

BEINGS OF LIGHT

15

NORDIC "NAZI" ALIEN

17

SAGASHA UFONAUT

19

DIANE SHE CAME FROM VENUS

ASHTAR COMMAND REPRESENTATIVE

© Carol Ann Rodriguez

THE GREYS

25

A NIGHT TIME VISITOR IN TIMMY'S WINDOW

27

ST GERMAIN THE MAN FROM TELOS

29

ANGEL-LIKE ALIENS COME TO GUIDE AND PROTECT

31

© Carol Ann Rodriguez

OFF TO NEVER, NEVER, LAND

33

WINGED VISITOR FROM "SATURN"

35

TELOS MAGICAL CITY BENEATH MT SHASTA

© Carol Ann Rodriguez

FRIENDLY PEOPLE OF THE INNER EARTH

BENEVOLENT VISITOR

CRYSTAL MAGIC

43

A WHOLE NEW WORLD AWAITS © Carol Ann Rodriguez

SAFE HARBOR

45

FAIRY DIMENSION

RAINBOW POWER

© Carol Ann Rodriguez

STAR GODS

© Carol Ann Rodriguez

STAR FLEET

© Carol Ann Rodriguez

DIAMOND IN THE SKY

© Carol Ann Rodriguez

CENTURIAN SCOUTS

© Carol Ann Rodriguez

THE FOUNDING OF A NATION

59

HOLD THAT TIGER

USO - UNIDENTIFIED SUBMERGED OBJECT

63

MR UNICORN

PYRAMID POWER

© Carol Ann Rodriguez

BLOWING IN THE WIND, AIR ELEMENTAL

© Carol Ann Rodriguez

FACE ON MARS

71

INVADING FORCES

73

THE BLEU MAN

MEN-IN-BLACK

77

FIRE BREATHING DRAGON

© Carol Ann Rodriguez

IN SEARCH OF LOST WORLDS

© Carol Ann Rodriguez

THE DERO

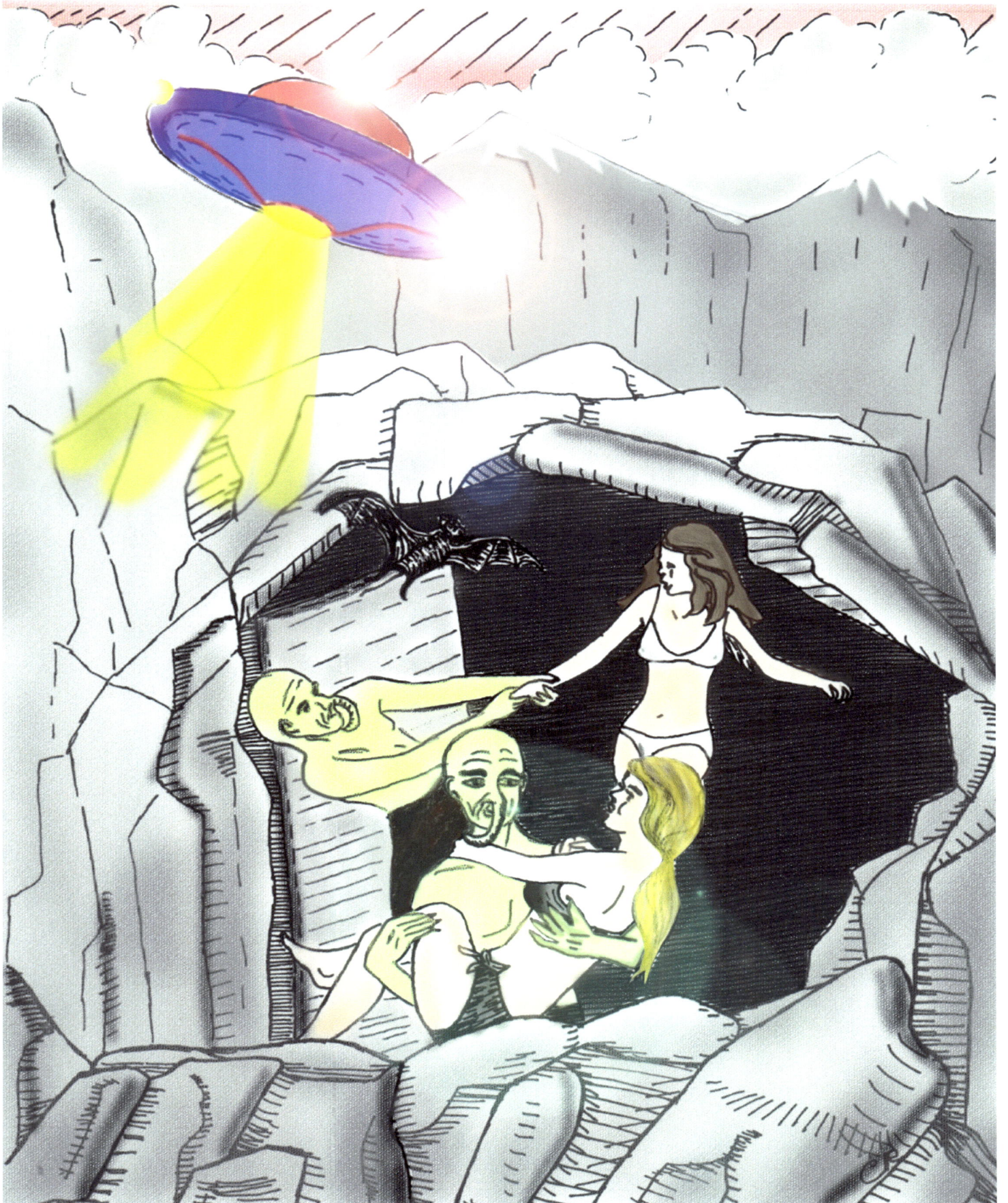

© Carol Ann Rodriguez

GUARDIAN OF THE PIRATE'S TREASURE

85

BATS JUST WANT TO HAVE FUN

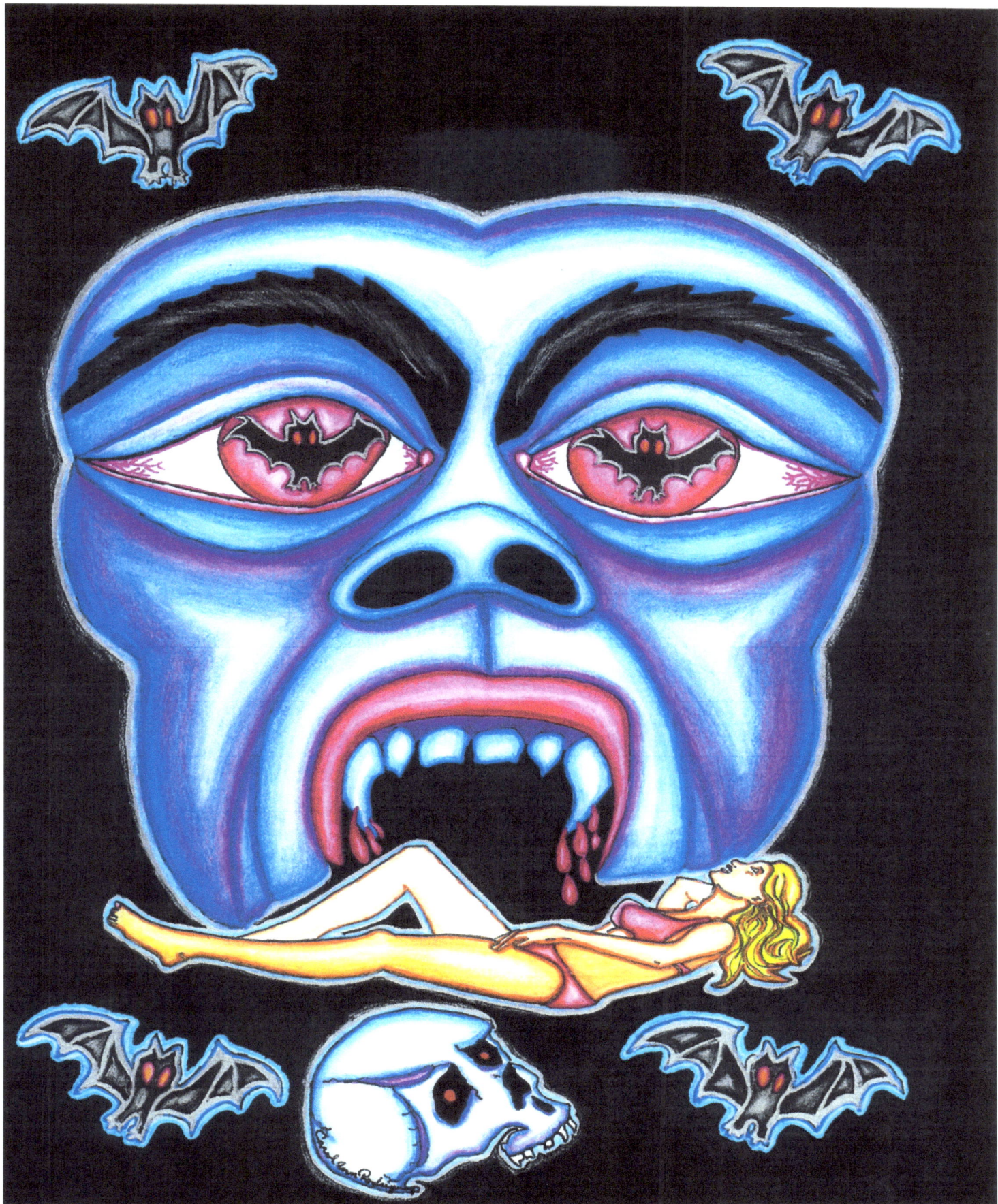

© Carol Ann Rodriguez

87

MIDNIGHT MEETING AT DRACULA'S CASTLE

89

© Carol Ann Rodriguez

HAUNTED HOUSE ON THE EDGE OF TIME

© Carol Ann Rodriguez

RIP - WE LOVE YOU ALL!

TIM AND CAROL INSIDE MOTHERSHIP OVER YUCATAN.
FROM PRIVATE COLLECTION   © Carol Ann Rodriguez

For a FREE catalog of books, videos and other fascinating items, send us your mailing address to:

Inner Light/Global Communications
P.O. Box 753
New Brunswick, NJ 08903

Email: mrufo8@hotmail.com

Conspiracyjournal.com

YouTube Channel – Mr UFOs Secret Files